Food
watch

Written by
MARTYN BRAMWELL
Consultant
CATRIONA LENNOX

A Dorling Kindersley Book

**Dorling** DK **Kindersley**

LONDON, NEW YORK, SYDNEY, DELHI,
PARIS, MUNICH, and JOHANNESBURG

Project Editor Jane Yorke
Senior Art Editor Marcus James
Senior Editor Fran Jones
Managing Editor Sue Grabham
Senior Managing Art Editor Julia Harris
Picture Researcher Samantha Nunn
Production Nicola Torode and Jenny Jacoby
DTP Designer Nomazwe Madonko
US Editor Margaret Parrish

First American Edition, 2001
00 01 02 03 04 05 10 9 8 7 6 5 4 3 2 1

Published in the United States by
Dorling Kindersley Publishing Inc.
95 Madison Avenue
New York, New York 10016

Copyright © 2001 Dorling Kindersley Limited

The CIP record for this book is available
from the Library of Congress

ISBN 0-7894-7765-3

Reproduced by Colourscan, Singapore
Printed and bound by L.E.G.O., Italy

See our complete catalog at

www.dk.com

Contents

Introduction

Many of us take our food for granted and sit down to a meal without really considering where the food comes from. Elsewhere, millions of people are not so fortunate – they have to do without and go hungry. Providing the world's growing population with enough food and clean water are two of the biggest problems facing governments and scientists today.

In the developed world, farming is big business, and most farmers benefit from fertile soils, mild climates, and enough income to invest in machinery, good-quality seed, and pesticides and fertilizers to improve their crops. Many farms are so productive that people grow more food than they need, but there is a cost to the environment. Intensive farming methods and overuse of chemicals can pollute the land and rivers and drive out the wild plants, insects, birds, and animals that inhabit the countryside.

In the developing world, it is a very different story. Millions of individual farmers struggle to make a living from infertile soils in regions plagued by drought or, the opposite extreme, floods. Vulnerable soils are being damaged by desperate people grazing too many livestock or cutting down trees for firewood. Rural populations are moving to the cities, where they face additional problems – overcrowded slums, polluted water and poor sanitation, unemployment, poor health, and a lack of education. At the heart of this crisis is poverty. Without jobs, the world's poor cannot afford to buy food.

However, solutions to many of these problems are available. Scientists are developing new varieties of crop plants that can resist diseases or survive droughts. Ruined soil is being brought back to life with the help of irrigation and the planting of trees and grasses. Many farmers are taking better care of the environment, and some are adopting organic methods to grow healthy crops. On some of the main issues, such as genetically modified food, experts do not always agree on what should be done. This book explains both sides of the argument and presents a clear picture of what is at stake.

> **"Worldwide, enough food is produced to feed everyone, yet this food and the technology to produce it do not always reach those in need."**
>
> NAFIS SADIK, EXECUTIVE DIRECTOR
> THE UNITED NATIONS FUND FOR POPULATION ACTIVITIES

Because the world food crisis is so big, it is easy to feel that there is little we can do. But individuals can make a difference. In this book, there are suggestions for ways you can play an active role, as well as experiments to provide firsthand experience of some of the scientific issues. Day in the life journals describe the work of experts in the field, while letters from young people around the world reveal their concerns for the environment. If we act now, we can all help to safeguard the future of food.

FEEDING THE
WORLD

WORLDWIDE, FARMERS PRODUCE ENOUGH
FOOD TO FEED EVERYONE ON THE PLANET,
BUT IT DOES NOT ALWAYS REACH THOSE WHO NEED
it most. People in rich countries are supplied with too much
food while those in developing countries do not have enough.
As the world's population increases, ways must be found to
ensure that people can grow enough food to feed themselves

"The right to food is the most fundamental of all human rights."

JACQUES DIOUF 1999
DIRECTOR GENERAL OF THE UNITED NATIONS FOOD AND AGRICULTURE ORGANIZATION

Like these market customers in Madeira, in the Canary Islands (main picture), most people living in developed countries have plenty to eat and can afford to buy a variety of fresh, healthy foods. In famine-stricken Somalia (inset), it's another world. This child has to survive on just one meal a day – a thin porridge of cornmeal – provided by international aid.

Hungry Planet

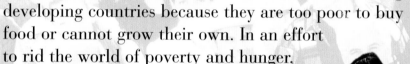

T hree babies are born every second, increasing the world's population by nearly 80 million every year. All these people need feeding. Most people living in rich countries have access to a wide selection of healthy foods. Meanwhile, millions go hungry in developing countries because they are too poor to buy food or cannot grow their own. In an effort to rid the world of poverty and hunger, politicians worldwide are seeking ways to educate their people, create new jobs, and boost low incomes. Better management of farmland and water resources is also helping to increase the world's production of food.

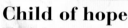

Child of hope

This baby boy was born in October 1999 in the city of Sarajevo. The United Nations chose him to symbolize the world's six billionth person and hope for a future free from war, poverty, and hunger.

Free lunch

In many developing countries, schools and church organizations play an important part in making sure that young people are properly fed. These school children in West Bengal, India are tucking into a meal of rice and vegetables, paid for by the education system. Many schools also teach local women about the importance of hygiene and a good diet in raising strong, healthy children.

Rice is eaten as the main part of most Asian meals.

Food sources

Plants are the source of all our food. Farmers around the world grow different plants either as food crops or to feed to animals, which are reared for their meat. A healthy, well-balanced diet should provide the carbohydrates, proteins, vitamins, and minerals necessary for growth and fighting disease.

Grains
Most people get their basic food energy from grains like wheat, rice, and maize.

One meal a day

In the hot, dry regions of Africa, finding enough firewood to cook just one hot meal a day is a big problem. This woman in Burkina Faso is cooking over an open fire, but in many areas simple stoves are being introduced. These use the scarce fuel much more efficiently, improving life for the people and causing less environmental damage.

Supermarket choice

An average supermarket has about 40,000 different food items on its shelves. Only a few products will be home-grown, many more – from fresh fruit to dried, frozen, and canned goods – originate from abroad, and require energy for transportation, freezers, and cold stores. Most supermarkets now stock a growing range of foods that label where the food is produced.

> **"It's my conviction that there is no reason not to have a hunger-free world some time in the next century."**

JACQUES DIOUF 1999
DIRECTOR-GENERAL OF THE UNITED NATIONS
FOOD AND AGRICULTURE ORGANIZATION

Waste not, want not

Pie-eating contests are fun, but only rich people living in developed countries can afford to waste food. Tonnes of unwanted food and packaging are thrown away every day. Getting rid of this huge amount of rubbish is an expensive and difficult problem.

Fruit and vegetables
Fresh fruit and vegetables are a valuable source of vitamins and minerals.

Poultry
Chickens, geese, turkeys, and ducks are reared for their eggs and meat.

Fish
Most fish and shellfish are caught from the sea. Some types of fish can be farmed.

Livestock
Cattle, sheep, and pigs are reared for their meat. Cows are farmed for their milk.

Uneven

Poor harvest

Farmers in many developing countries suffer poor harvests from their dry, infertile soils. Fertilizers can help, but they are expensive, and many farmers rely on supplies donated by aid agencies. Lack of money also means that almost all of the farm labor must be carried out by hand.

Farmers have the means of producing more food while still protecting the environment

F armers in the rich and fertile regions of the world are fortunate because they can produce an abundance of food. Even if their crops are not needed immediately, the harvests can be preserved and sold later. However, excess fresh food often goes to waste because it is unwanted where it is grown. In contrast, farmers in the world's poorest countries struggle with infertile soils and a lack of water for little return. When their crops fail they have no money to buy imported food. Governments are helping these farmers to become self-sufficient by teaching them more productive land-use methods.

Rich harvest

A bumper crop of sweet peppers pours into a trailer behind a harvester on a farm in California. This is "intensive" farming – producing very high yields by using modern methods. Soil fertility has been boosted by fertilizers, and chemical sprays have kept pests and crop diseases away. The high value of the crop provides the profits the farmer needs to invest in expensive harvesting machines and agricultural chemicals.

Harvest

Preserving the food

Developed countries have many ways of preserving food so that it remains in perfect condition for months or even years. Food processing and packaging enables supermarkets to stock their shelves all year round. It also allows producers to export foods to other rich countries.

Bottling
Pickled tomatoes, pickles, even eggs, can be stored in air-tight jars like this.

Freezing
Fruit and vegetables, like these peas, can be washed, frozen, and packed within hours of being picked on the farm.

Canning
Fruit, fish, beans, and many other foods will last for years in sealed metal cans.

Smoking
For thousands of years, people have preserved fish and meat by smoking.

Drying
Sun- or machine-dried fruits keep their flavor and nutritional value.

Storage problems

In parts of Africa, up to a quarter of all stored grain is damaged by mold, weevils, or rodents. This raised corn store in KwaZulu-Natal, South Africa, is the only way farmers can store their precious corn harvest. Many international aid programs are helping villagers to design and build better storage containers.

> Halving the **amount** lost in storage could **save** more than **30 million** tons of **grain** a year

Rodent pests
Rats and mice eat tons of stored grain every year.

What a waste!

Modern agriculture is so productive that sometimes harvests are too big to be consumed. Here, unwanted California oranges are dumped and left to rot on the ground. In Europe, surplus milk is sometimes emptied down old mine shafts. Unfortunately, it is too costly to transport this excess food to places in the world where people are hungry.

FAMINE!

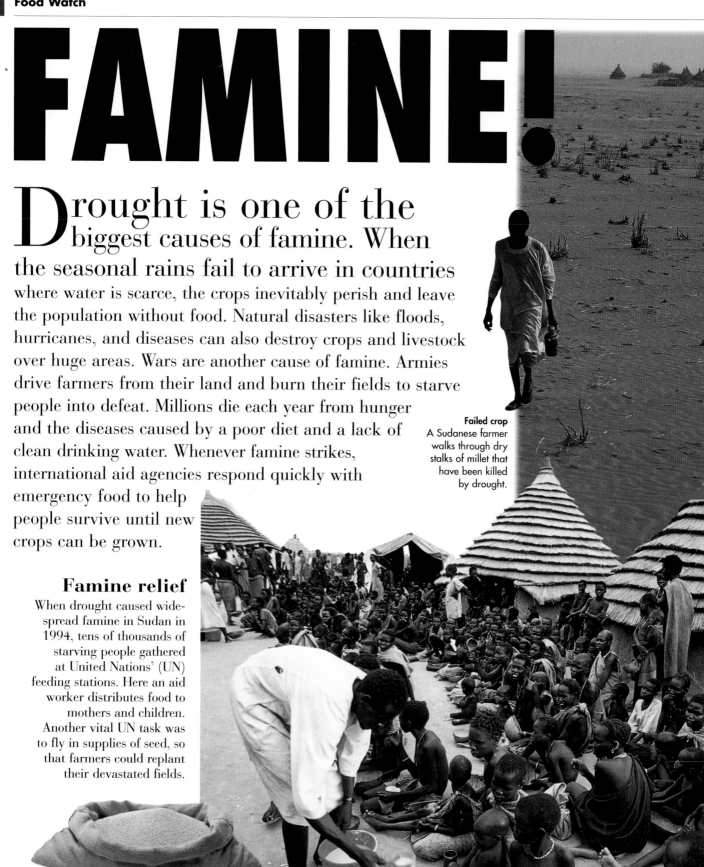

Drought is one of the biggest causes of famine. When the seasonal rains fail to arrive in countries where water is scarce, the crops inevitably perish and leave the population without food. Natural disasters like floods, hurricanes, and diseases can also destroy crops and livestock over huge areas. Wars are another cause of famine. Armies drive farmers from their land and burn their fields to starve people into defeat. Millions die each year from hunger and the diseases caused by a poor diet and a lack of clean drinking water. Whenever famine strikes, international aid agencies respond quickly with emergency food to help people survive until new crops can be grown.

Failed crop
A Sudanese farmer walks through dry stalks of millet that have been killed by drought.

Famine relief

When drought caused wide-spread famine in Sudan in 1994, tens of thousands of starving people gathered at United Nations' (UN) feeding stations. Here an aid worker distributes food to mothers and children. Another vital UN task was to fly in supplies of seed, so that farmers could replant their devastated fields.

Food aid
Cereals like millet are ideal for emergency food aid. They are high in food energy and are easy to transport.

Loading aid supplies
Grain sacks are loaded onto sliding palettes that can be pushed out of the plane's rear doors.

Drop zone
The food drop is done at low speed and altitude. Some sacks will burst, but the grain can be gathered up unharmed.

Airborne aid

An air drop from a cargo plane is often the only way to get emergency food quickly to the victims of famine. Before food supplies can be transported overland, large numbers of trucks and gasoline need to be available. Even then, the going can be slow and difficult in disaster areas, where roads have become impassable.

Flooded farmland

Disaster struck in 1999, when two hurricanes hit the coastal state of Orissa in southeast India. Storm winds and floods killed 8,000, left millions homeless, and destroyed crops over a wide area. Once floodwaters subside, fields covered by muddy river water recover quickly, but the salt from seawater creates longer-term damage to the soil.

"In 1999, the World Food Program fed more than 86 million people in 82 countries."

THE UNITED NATIONS
WORLD FOOD PROGRAM

ACTION!
FAMINE RELIEF

Take part in a sponsored event to raise funds for famine victims.

Watch the news and discuss famine issues at school or with friends.

Give a week's allowance to a good cause.

Refugee crisis

In 1999, thousands of people were forced to flee their homes to escape from the fierce fighting in Kosovo. Many of the war refugees became trapped in the countryside with no means of obtaining food. Aid agencies used helicopters to deliver bread and other foodstuffs to groups of hungry refugees.

NUTRITIONIST
HENERIETTA HOWARD

HENERIETTA HOWARD IS A NUTRITIONIST AND NURSE WORKING FOR MEDECINS SANS FRONTIERES (MSF) – DOCTORS WITHOUT BORDERS – IN THE TOWN OF Konso, southern Ethiopia, Africa. Henerietta coordinates a team of nurses who supply supplementary food to malnourished children and pregnant women in the local population.

A day in the life of a

NUTRITIONIST

The MSF supplementary food project is vital for those children suffering from malnutrition in drought-stricken southern Ethiopia.

Today, Henerietta will visit about 400 pregnant mothers and children at a food distribution site near Konso with a team of five people, including a nurse.

Land of drought
Much of southern Ethiopia is suffering the effects of severe drought.

Getting around
The teams travel cross-country in four-wheel-drive vehicles.

6:00am I get up early and have breakfast together with the MSF nurses in the Konso compound. We eat bread and injara (Ethiopian food), drink shai (tea), and talk about preparations for the day ahead. There are five teams in total, so I organize who's going to go to each of the different food distribution sites. Next we load the equipment and supplies of Faffa – a supplementary food powder consisting of corn and sorghum strengthened with proteins, vitamins, and minerals – into the cars. We all take a flask of water with us, as it gets very hot during the day. The nurses also fill up a large jerrican with clean water,

in case it's needed for their work, such as cleaning the eyes of children with conjunctivitis (an eye infection).

7:00am We leave the compound in four-wheel-drive vehicles. These are the most practical way of traveling around a region that has no real roads. The journey is bumpy and uncomfortable. Today my team is headed for the Fasha distribution site, not far from Konso.

Registration time
Henerietta fills out a detailed record for each person on the register.

8:00am When we get to Fasha, the pregnant mothers and children are already lined up waiting patiently for us. The people are kept calm by a crowd-control person, trained by MSF. These hardworking people are weak from lack of water and food. The rains have failed to arrive, which means the crops cannot grow in the fields, and there is no harvest to feed their families. The first task we perform is

Town of Konso
In good years, the rains arrive on time, and the people of southern Ethiopia are able to farm the land and feed their families. When the rains fail, the people rely on food aid from agencies like MSF.

to give health education to the mothers. This involves teaching them how to prepare the Faffa powder so that it can be eaten. We stress that Faffa is a supplementary food and should not form a child's main diet. We emphasize that the powder

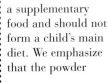

Weighing pants

Stethoscope

Medical equipment
The nurses use basic equipment to make their health checks.

should only be fed to the person who is registered with us as being malnourished. We also give health advice on the importance of personal hygiene and on how to prevent skin disorders such as scabies. Contagious diseases, such as diarrhea, are common among small children in the dry season, so we explain how to avoid passing them on to other people.

10:00am Our next task is to weigh the children – babies are placed in

Waiting for food
Pregnant women and mothers with small children often walk long distances to get help at the distribution sites.

the weighing pants – and measure their heights with a measuring board. Next I calculate the weight-to-height ratio for all children under five years of age. This is a way of checking that a child weighs enough for his or her height. Those who are medically underweight are registered to receive Faffa. I fill out all the details in the registration book. Meanwhile, the nurse carries out the medical screening of the children, giving basic health care if necessary. Children often suffer from a dry mouth and tongue because they have had no water to drink for a long time. The nurse gives these children a cup of water from the jerrican. We also give Faffa to women who are seven or more months pregnant or who are breast-feeding their babies.

12:00pm The last part of the process involves distributing the Faffa, which looks like huge white bags of flour. The powder is measured out with a measuring cup and 4.5 lb (2 kg) of Faffa is put into each mother's special bag. The women used to carry away the powder in odd pieces of cloth or old plastic bags but now we've handed out special orange resealing Faffa bags. These bags can be cleaned out and brought back each week for reusing. We are very strict, and if the women

forget their bag, they do not get their ration of Faffa.

3:00pm Before the end of the day, after we've seen around 300 women and children, we rest and drink a little. Sometimes we have to go the whole day without food because it's just too busy. We always treat the mothers and children who arrive late – some of them have to walk a very long way to get to the distribution site.

4:00pm Finally, it's time to pack up our equipment and return to the compound. Sometimes we take any severely malnourished children back with us, so that they can get urgent medical help at the hospital in Konso.

5:00pm I take a quick shower, and then we have our dinner together. The teams discuss how the day went and share their experiences, trying to find solutions to any problems that have arisen. It's very rewarding being in Ethiopia. During the war in Liberia, MSF helped my people so now I feel that I should help others in need in return. I really feel for the Ethiopian people, who work hard and pray for the rains to come. My work is very tiring, but the reward I get is bringing malnourished children back to life. Thanks to the work of MSF, many children are able to survive the drought in this dry, brittle land.

" Every week, we give Faffa to about 10,000 people in southern Ethiopia – which is a lot, and the malnutrition problem is getting worse. **"**

Faffa distribution
A measured amount of Faffa powder is given to each mother.

Costing the
EARTH

$\mathbf{M}$uch of the food on sale today has been packed, processed or preserved, and shipped halfway around the world. However, there's a high environmental price to pay for all of this food choice. Processing and transporting food uses large amounts of energy, and creates problems such as pollution and waste. Also, fragile habitats are being destroyed by small farmers trying to earn a living by producing crops and livestock for export.

Hidden costs

The burger has become the world's favorite snack and millions are eaten every day. More than 20 different ingredients are needed to make one burger. These ingredients come from farmers around the world. This convenience food is cheap to buy, but consumers might be wise to think about how it is produced.

Bread bun
Large amounts of energy are needed to process foods such as bread and mayonnaise.

Beef burger
Beef is reared cheaply in developing countries and exported long distances.

Salad garnish
Farmers spray pesticides on lettuces and tomatoes to be sure of good harvests.

Environmental destruction

Much of the beef for America's burgers is imported from Brazil. Here large areas of the Amazon rain forest have been cut down to make way for cattle ranches. The thin soil can only support grazing for a few years, and the land quickly becomes bare, eroded, and ruined.

RIPENING BANANAS

You will need: 2 unripe bananas, 1 ripe banana, 2 polyethylene food bags, 2 bag ties.

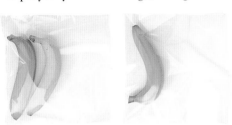

1 PLACE ONE UNRIPE (green) banana in a bag along with the ripe one. Place the second unripe banana in a bag on its own.

2 SEAL BOTH BAGS with the ties. Leave the bananas on a sunny windowsill or in a warm place for a few days.

3 LOOK AT THE bananas after two or three days. The unripe banana bagged with the ripe one will ripen faster than the unripe banana on its own.

This shows that: ripening fruit gives off a gas – ethylene – which triggers fruit to ripen. The gas is used in warehouses to ripen fruit that has been picked "green" and chilled for export.

Storage and supply costs

Supermarkets use vast amounts of electricity to run their lights, freezer cabinets, and cold stores. Great quantities of fuel are also needed for the ships, planes, and trucks that travel long distances to supply the stores. The resulting air pollution from exhaust fumes is one of the major causes of climate change.

Food processing

Most of the fresh produce grown on farms is processed and packaged in factories before it ends up on the supermarket shelf. The production of ready-to-eat meals and long-life foods provides large numbers of people with jobs, but it makes food more expensive.

Recycling waste

Recycling is just one of the alternatives to burying trash. Many cities are building recycling facilities, which reuse the packaging people throw away. If materials are recycled, fewer minerals need to be dug from the ground and fewer trees have to be cut down, which can only be good for the environment.

Glass
Bottles and jars are melted down to make new glass products.

Plastics
Manufacturers need to do more research into ways of recycling plastics.

Paper
Recycling paper and cardboard saves trees and preserves forests.

Metals
Recycling aluminum and steel cans uses less energy than making new ones.

Garbage mountains

Tons of discarded food packaging and household waste are thrown away each week. The garbage often ends up in pits in the ground, where it is packed down and covered with dirt. This solution is not ideal, since the rotting waste can produce chemicals that pollute groundwater or give off foul-smelling gases.

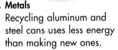

Crops for **Cash**

Crops that farmers grow specially to be sold abroad are known as cash crops. They earn money for a country needing to buy goods that it does not have, such as fuel oil or machinery. Cash crops include produce such as bananas, coffee, and soybeans, as well as nonfood products such as cotton and rubber. This system can work well but can also leave the farming community vulnerable. If there is a crop disease or natural disaster, such as a hurricane, the crop can be lost and there is no other farming to fall back on. Also, growing the same crop year after year can exhaust the soil by removing all its nutrients. Today, most countries try not to rely on just one crop.

The bananas are picked green for export.

Crop power

Bananas are the main export crop of St. Lucia in the Caribbean. In the past, the banana trade in this region was controlled by big companies and supermarkets, who paid poor prices for the produce. However, banana producers and small growers have joined forces in recent times and pressed these companies into paying fairer prices for their fruit.

❝ My name is Rayan and I live in St Lucia, where the main crop is bananas. In the hurricane season, my parents – with other plantation workers – are worried because hurricanes can destroy entire crops. I remember when a tropical depression hit St. Lucia in 1994. All the crops were destroyed and most kids could not go to school because their parents were unemployed and there was no other source of income. Food was also a problem, as bananas are one of the basic foods that most poor families survive on because you get them free. ❞ *Rayan Charlery*

Natural disaster

This is what Hurricane Mitch did to a banana plantation in Honduras in 1998. The entire plantation was destroyed and it will take years to establish a new one. Countries that depend heavily on just one or two main export crops suffer very badly when one of their money-earners is wiped out by storm, flood, or disease.

Crops for animals

Huge farms in Brazil are devoted to producing soybean crops for export as animal feed, rather than producing food for the local population. Farming on this scale requires large amounts of fertilizer to make the plants grow and pesticides to control the diseases that spread easily through a single crop.

Soybeans

Soybean pods

Large-scale agriculture

In Sri Lanka, the large tea plantations are harvested by hand. The young tea leaves are picked from the bushes, then dried, crushed, and packed for export. Cash crops, like tea, often take up much of a country's best land, although in many places food crops are grown alongside them. When the vegetation is cleared to grow cash crops, some native animals can lose both their natural habitat and their food supplies.

Tea terraces occupy a large proportion of fertile farmland in Asia.

Balanced harvest

This Indonesian market has a huge variety of homegrown fruits, vegetables, and spices on sale. The crops are grown alongside the country's main cash crops – coffee, tea, sugar, rubber, palm oil, and tobacco – on both small family farms and large commercial plantations. Indonesia has a strong agricultural economy thanks to the balanced farming of both cash and food crops.

FARMING THE EARTH

FOR THOUSANDS OF YEARS, PEOPLE HAVE BEEN CUTTING DOWN FORESTS AND PLOWING UP LAND TO GROW CROPS and rear animals. Overfarming around the world has led to the loss of fertile soil, the pollution of rivers, and the extinction of wildlife. Today, farmers are learning how to produce enough food without disturbing the delicate balance of nature.

> **66** The increased food required to meet the needs of twice as many people must come largely from better use of the land already farmed. **99**
>
> **"CARING FOR THE EARTH"**
> **WORLD CONSERVATION UNION/ UNITED NATIONS ENVIRONMENT PROGRAM/ WORLDWIDE FUND FOR NATURE**

This green and fertile farmland in England (main picture) is divided up by hedgerows and trees, which can provide precious shelter for local wildlife. In stark contrast, much of the farmland in Sudan (inset) is dry and barren – a situation caused by the overgrazing of animals and the loss of trees and plants.

Soil is the most efficient recycling system on Earth

Rich Soil, Poor Soil

The most precious natural resource on the planet is not gold or oil, but the earth beneath our feet. Soil is not just "dirt," it's a mixture of rock fragments, air, water, and the decaying remains of plants and animals. It teems with tiny creatures that mix and process the soil, and keep it healthy. Some soils are very fertile, others are not, but they support all other life on Earth – from the Amazon rain forest to the Arctic tundra. It is important that farmers use the soil carefully and protect the wheat fields, rice paddies, orchards, and market gardens that feed the world's people.

Dead plant and animal remains on the soil surface are called "litter."

Worms, grubs, and insects chew up the litter and drag it into the soil.

Bacteria and fungi convert the litter into humus and nutrients.

Earthworks

A field can hold several billion worms, mites, millipedes, fungi, and bacteria. This hidden workforce breaks down the remains of dead plants and animals into nutrients – chemicals that can be reused by growing plants – and humus, which binds the soil together and helps to hold in moisture.

Larger rock fragments and cracks in the solid rock below, allow excess water to drain away.

Fertile soil

Many European farmers keep their land fertile by plowing the unwanted stems and roots of a harvested crop back into the soil. Here, the remaining stubble (stalks) of a grain crop will provide much needed nutrients and humus for the next season's crop. It is the humus that gives this soil its rich, dark color.

Reviving soil

In the deserts of Morocco, farmers have to channel water to their fields from deep boreholes nearby. Water irrigation helps to turn dusty, infertile soil into farmland. By digging in plant matter, farmers can fertilize and strengthen the soil. The added humus reduces wind erosion and holds precious moisture around the roots of crops.

Nodules on bean roots

Fertilizer factories

Plants need nitrogen for growth, but many soils don't contain enough. Farmers can help by planting peas, beans, or clover. These plants have nodules (lumps) on their roots containing bacteria that capture nitrogen from the air in the soil. This is turned into a kind of nitrogen fertilizer that plants can take in through their roots.

Infertile soil

Farmers work hard to cultivate the poor soil on farms in the Turkish highlands, where winters are very cold and summers are very hot. The soil is thin, dry, and stony, and its pale color shows that it contains very little humus. Infertile soils can be improved without the use of chemical fertilizers by adding animal manure.

WHAT LIVES IN SOIL? *EXPERIMENT*

You will need: damp soil, trowel, kitchen sieve, funnel, large clean jar, saucer, small paint brush, desk lamp, magnifying glass.

1 PUT A SMALL amount of damp garden soil carefully into the sieve.

2 PLACE THE SIEVE in the funnel and place the funnel in the jar. Position the lamp above the soil. Switch on the lamp and leave for a few hours. As the soil dries out, any tiny animals will move away from the heat until they drop through the funnel into the jar.

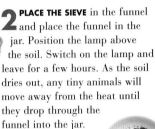

3 SWITCH OFF THE LAMP and remove the sieve and funnel. Tip the contents of the jar into the saucer and use the brush to separate out the tiny animals from the soil. Examine the creatures closely with your magnifying glass.

This shows that: tiny animals live in soil. They keep soil healthy by breaking down the remains of dead plants so that their nutrients can be used again.

Always wash your hands after handling soil.

The soil washed off the island of Java each year would grow enough food for 15 million people

Soil erosion

This Mexican valley was not wrecked by earthquakes or by miners, but by sheep. Farmers have allowed their flocks to overgraze the land but have not given the grass time to recover. Without its protective carpet of grass and roots to anchor it to the hillside, the precious soil has been eroded (washed away) by rain in a matter of months.

Working with the Land

Eco-friendly fields

This patchwork of fields in Norway shows how modern farms can work in harmony with the natural landscape. Farmers have preserved the hedgerows and patches of woodland. These will provide homes for the insects that pollinate their crops as well as the hunting birds and mammals that help to control pests.

All around the world, farmers have found successful ways of raising crops and livestock in the most unlikely places. Many of these traditional methods do not require expensive machines or chemicals, they simply make the best use of the local conditions. Some of the farming techniques have been in use for thousands of years – mostly without damaging the environment.

The hillside terraces prevent heavy rain from washing away the thin mountain soil.

Terracing the hillsides

The terraced rice fields of Asia show the wisdom of ancient farmers. Rainwater collects on the narrow fields and the overflow slowly trickles downhill from terrace to terrace. Any precious soil particles carried in the water simply end up on the ledge below. Some hill terraces have been in use for more than 2,000 years.

Farming on the move

In desert and semi-desert areas, many livestock herders, like this Afghan goat herder, live a nomadic way of life – constantly moving from one patch of sparse grazing to the next. This works with small numbers of animals, but in parts of east Africa grazing too many animals has turned areas from wooded grassland into barren desert.

Overgrazing leaves the soil bare and at risk of being blown away by the wind or washed away by the rain.

Shifting agriculture

These Peruvian rain forest farmers are planting a cassava crop after clearing a patch of forest. The felled trees have been burned to fertilize the soil with ash. This small farming family will use the plot for a few years, then move on. This method of farming can damage the rain forest if it's cut too often and has no time to grow back.

Traditional farmers around the globe know their land intimately, and what it can support

Stone walls hold back the water needed for growing rice.

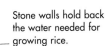

Hill farming

Sheep farmers in Devon, England, graze their flocks on the upland pastures. This is the only way of using hillsides where soils are thin and the vegetation consists of short-stemmed grasses. Cattle are less hardy and can only eat long-stemmed grasses in lower pastures. Farmers often have to provide extra feed in winter, or bring the sheep down into the warmer valleys.

" I live on a hill farm in Yorkshire, England. My father has a flock of 950 Swaledale sheep which graze up on the hills called the moors. The sheep can survive the cold, heavy rain, and snow. My father takes extra feed and hay up to the sheep in the winter months. In April, I go with my family and our two sheepdogs up onto the moors to gather the sheep and bring them down for lambing. This takes three or four days because the moors are so big. The lambs are born in the fields, where we can care for them. "

Jenny Harker

Carbon dioxide gas enters through pores (tiny holes) in the leaves.

Excess oxygen is given off into the atmosphere.

Growing

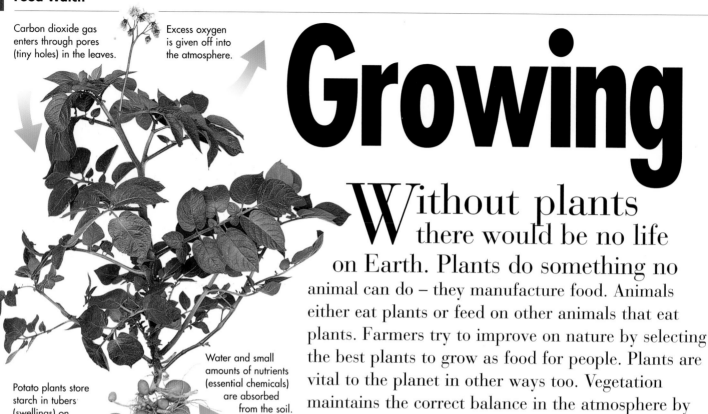

Potato plants store starch in tubers (swellings) on underground stems.

Water and small amounts of nutrients (essential chemicals) are absorbed from the soil.

W Without plants
there would be no life on Earth. Plants do something no animal can do – they manufacture food. Animals either eat plants or feed on other animals that eat plants. Farmers try to improve on nature by selecting the best plants to grow as food for people. Plants are vital to the planet in other ways too. Vegetation maintains the correct balance in the atmosphere by absorbing carbon dioxide and giving off the oxygen that animals need to breathe. Plants also benefit the environment, as their roots bind the soil together, preventing water loss and land erosion.

Food factory

A plant grows by using the energy in sunlight to drive a chemical process called photosynthesis. Water and nutrients are drawn up from the soil by the roots, and carbon dioxide gas from the air is taken in through the leaves. These chemicals are broken down into carbon, hydrogen, and oxygen and then recombined to make sugars and starches, the main components of food.

Seeds
Peas and beans are nutritious foods. The plants also improve soils.

Fruits
Fruits are a rich source of sugar and fiber for people and animals.

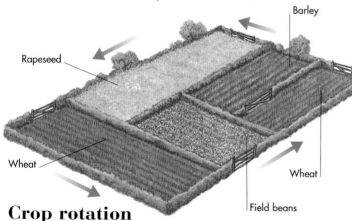

Barley

Rapeseed

Wheat

Wheat

Field beans

Leaves
Plant leaves are food for animals and people, and also make natural compost.

Roots
Cassava and other starchy roots are important food crops.

Crop rotation

Some plants take a lot of nutrients from the soil, so if the same crop is grown year after year, the soil can lose its fertility. Other crops, such as peas and beans, actually put nutrients back. Many farmers keep their soil healthy by using a rotation system. They change the crops that they grow in the same field each year.

Food stores

Plants use some of the sugar they make as fuel to keep their life-support systems going. The rest is converted into either cellulose for making new plant cells, or starch, which is stored as food for next year's seeds and shoots. Farmers harvest these food stores for people to eat.

Stems
Many plant stems are plowed under to fertilize the soil. Rhubarb stems are eaten.

Cycles

Warmth of the Sun

Farmers rely on sunlight to grow strong, healthy crops. Many have to time the growing season so that the crops are in leaf during the summer months when the daylight hours are long and the Sun is at its most powerful. Most plants grow well in normal daylight, but fruit trees, like those in this Brazilian orange orchard, need warm sunshine to ripen their fruit.

Life-giving rain

Mild, wet winters and warm summers create ideal farming conditions across much of America, Europe, and Asia. Most tropical countries have either too much rain, or too little – both problems are made worse by poor soils and unsuitable farming methods. These leave the land exposed to floods, or to soil erosion, which can turn the land into desert.

Global warming

Pollution from factory smoke, car exhausts, and damaging chemicals is upsetting the balance of the atmosphere and causing the Earth to warm up. Higher temperatures mean sea levels are rising and this puts coastal areas at risk of flooding. Future changes in world temperatures and rainfall patterns may affect the crops that farmers can grow, and where they can grow them.

Flood barriers
In Bangladesh, farmers reinforce river banks and coastlines to protect their fields from floodwaters.

GERMINATING WATERCRESS *EXPERIMENT*

You will need: watercress or mustard seeds, 3 plastic cups, cotton balls, small box, water.

1 FILL TWO-THIRDS of each plastic cup with cotton balls. Sprinkle some watercress seeds on top.

2 POUR A LITTLE water into two of the cups to dampen the cotton. Fill the third cup to the brim, so that the seeds are kept underwater and get no air.

3 PLACE ONE OF the cups with damp cotton in the dark, inside a box. Place the other two cups on a sunny windowsill.

4 WATER ALL THE SEEDS each day. After five days, compare the seeds in the different cups. Only the seeds exposed to the air on damp cotton will have germinated (sprouted). The seeds kept in the dark will be weak, yellow plants, while those kept in the light will be strong and bright green.

This shows that: seeds need just the right conditions of moisture, sunlight, air, and warmth in order to germinate and grow into strong, healthy plants.

The Feed MACHINE

In Canada, summer **wheat** harvests are 25 percent **bigger** in areas where there are natural **windbreaks**

Only farming on a huge scale can produce the vast amounts of grain and crops needed for human food and animal feed. But this kind of farming can have a large impact on the environment. When trees and bushes are removed to make way for giant farm machines, the soil and crops are left with no protection from the wind, and local wildlife can lose their homes. The chemicals used to fertilize the soil and control pests and diseases may also cause harm by poisoning innocent species and by leaking into nearby rivers.

Grain production

In Oregon, the wheat crop is harvested with combine harvesters. These giant machines provide the most efficient way of harvesting grain crops from huge fields. However, these large engines are powered by diesel fuel which pollutes the atmosphere. Originally thought to be less polluting than gasoline, scientists have now confirmed that the opposite is true.

Wind damage

In some parts of the world, a serious environmental problem with very large fields is that once the crop is harvested, the soil is left bare and vulnerable. In long spells of hot weather, the precious topsoil soon dries out. A strong wind can blow away hundreds of tons of soil in a matter of hours.

Hedge hideaway

Hedgerows on farm land help to preserve the environment. The dense foliage shields crops and soil from wind damage, and the tangled roots help to anchor the soil and conserve water. Hedges are the last stronghold of many rare wild flowers. They also provide living spaces for various species of insects, birds, reptiles, and mammals.

Red Admiral butterflies lay eggs on nettles, the main food of their caterpillars.

Blue tits nest in hedges and feed their young on grubs and caterpillars.

Rabbits burrow into banks and under hedges.

A typical **hedge** can support **20 bird** species and 50-60 different **plants**

Chemical spraying

Many people worry about the number of chemicals used on farms. Crops may be sprayed with fertilizers to help them grow well, herbicides to kill weeds, fungicides to stop molds, and insecticides to control harmful insects. But people cannot have it both ways. It is chemicals such as these that provide us with large, unblemished fruits and vegetables at reasonable prices.

ACTION!
SAVE WILDLIFE

Support organizations that encourage more wildlife in the countryside.

Join a group of volunteers to keep local hedges clear of litter.

Find out how organic food is grown without the use of chemicals.

Even delicate crops like tomatoes can be harvested by machine.

Clever machines

Specialized machines, like this tomato harvester, have replaced most of the people who once worked on farms in developed countries. They are expensive, but much faster than human workers. But heavy machines can damage the soil by packing it down so that air and water cannot pass through it freely. Most farm machines have huge balloon tires to minimize this problem.

Pest **Control**

Orchards, greenhouses, fields, and silos are under constant attack from rats and mice, seed-eating birds, and a host of bugs, beetles, worms, and grubs that bore into plant stems, chew their roots, nibble their leaves, and suck their sap. What's more, crops can also be invaded by a whole variety of diseases. In developed countries, farmers have come to rely on effective chemical sprays to combat these problems – but these can have a serious effect on the natural environment.

Barn owl
Chemicals in the mice caused the numbers of predator birds, such as owls, to fall.

Crop diseases

This corn (maize) cob is infected by maize smut – a disease caused by a fungus which covers the plant with masses of black, powdery spores. Other crops may be spoiled by rust, rot, or blight. This kills the leaves or tubers (underground swellings) and prevents the plants from growing.

Wheat
Farmers sprayed cereal crops with pesticides.

Field mouse
Mice ate the grain and stored deadly chemicals in their body fat.

Poisoned food chains

In the 1960s, scientists discovered that some pesticides were being passed along the food chain. Mice and small birds were eating the chemically treated seeds and, in turn, were preyed on by hawks and owls. The chemicals weakened the eggshells of the predator birds so that fewer chicks survived. This led to a decline in their species. Some of these chemicals, such as DDT, are now banned in many countries.

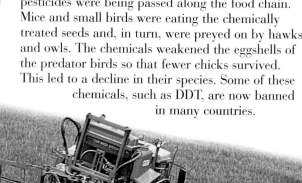

Unwelcome weeds

Poppies are not a problem for farmers, since the plants die before the grain is harvested. But other weeds can spoil the crop quality by using up valuable water and nutrients in the soil. Some choke and tangle the crop plants, or shade them from the sun. Farmers take great care to remove poisonous weeds from their fields.

Hungry pests

Crops are vulnerable to all sorts of pests. Slugs and snails eat the leaves of crop plants. Wireworms and other grubs bore into root vegetables, while insects attack the stems of plants to reach the sugar-rich sap. Many of these pests also spread diseases. Farmers control them with pesticides, but they have to be careful not to damage harmless insect species too.

A single snail can rapidly eat its way through a broccoli leaf.

My name is Woody, and I live in County Cork in Ireland. My family has a secret walled garden by the sea where we grow potatoes and corn-on-the-cob. When the vegetables start to grow, my brother Connie and I catch ladybugs and put them on the plants to eat the greenfly. We also put crushed eggshells and salt on the ground to stop slugs and snails from eating the leaves. We never use slug pellets because the songbirds might eat them and die.

Woody Cooper

"Biological control represents a natural, ecological approach to controlling pests and diseases."

BIOCONTROL OF PLANT DISEASES LABORATORY, UNITED STATES DEPARTMENT OF AGRICULTURE

Pesticide research

Scientists are constantly researching and testing more selective types of pesticides, designed to kill just the problem pest. However, weeds, insects, and crop diseases may eventually become resistant to the effects of farm chemicals, so new ones have to be developed all the time.

Farmers use long, boom sprays on tractors to mist-spray crops during the growing cycle.

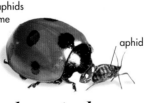

Natural predators
Ladybugs eat aphids and are welcome insects in farmers' fields.

aphid

Crop spraying

Many modern pesticides are designed to kill only the problem pest. Farmers use insecticides to remove insect pests, herbicides to kill weeds, and fungicides to prevent molds. Although most farmers only use the minimum amount of pesticides, some people are concerned about the levels of chemicals sprayed on food crops.

Biological control

Instead of relying on expensive chemicals to control insect pests, some farmers release one of the pest's natural enemies into their fields. For instance, ladybugs are used to keep down the numbers of aphids, and a tiny parasitic wasp can be used to control whitefly in greenhouses.

Fishing for **Food**

Competing for fish

Mauritanian fishers once had their coastal fishing grounds to themselves and were able to catch a plentiful supply of golden mullet. Today, these fishers have to compete with illegal trawlers from Europe and other far-off places. As well as reducing west Africa's fish stocks, the poachers are taking essential food from local people.

Fish provide people with a healthy source of food protein. In Japan, fish accounts for 60 percent of the protein people eat, and in rural parts of Africa, river and lake fish are often the only source of protein available. Small-scale local fishing does not harm the environment, but intensive fishing by deepwater trawlers in some areas is threatening to wipe out fish populations. Governments now put strict quotas or limits on the number of fish that can be caught in many fishing grounds. This action aims to conserve the world's endangered fish stocks for future generations.

Factory trawlers

The trawl nets used by this North Sea fishing boat can scoop up a ton of fish at a time. The nets used by deep-sea supertrawlers can take 100 tons in a single sweep. This devastating efficiency has caused some fish populations to fall dangerously low.

A winch is used to haul the bulging nets back on board.

Fish or forest?

Shrimp farming has provided a new source of food for people in Southeast Asia. The shrimp also command a good price when they are sold to wealthy countries. However, the creation of these fish ponds means cutting down coastal mangrove forests, which protect the shore and provide breeding grounds for other fish.

Mangrove trees protect the coast from erosion and storm damage.

Shrimp are cooked and frozen for export.

Shrimp farms now replace half of all Thailand's mangrove forests.

"**Of the 17 major fisheries in the world, 4 are depleted and 13 are either fished to capacity, or overfished**"

UNITED NATIONS FOOD AND AGRICULTURE ORGANIZATION 1995

ACTION!
PROTECT FISH

Only buy canned tuna marked "dolphin friendly" on the label – some tuna nets trap dolphins as well.

Discuss with your friends whether it makes sense to use so much fish as animal food.

Find out where the fish you eat comes from.

Fish meal industry

Do cows eat fish? Surprisingly, the answer is yes. And so do pigs, hens, and other farm animals. Nearly half of all the fish caught worldwide are processed into fish meal for use as animal feed. This factory in Peru helps to turn almost the whole of the country's fish catch into meal for the beef cattle of North America.

Traditional hunters

For centuries, sea mammals have provided the Inuit people of North America with the essentials of life – meat, skins for clothing, bones for harpoon heads, and blubber for lamps. Most Inuit now live in towns, but many still hunt in the traditional way. Some animal conservationists are demanding that these people give up their hunting rights.

Inuit cut holes in the sea ice to hunt seals.

SHELLY TALLACK COLLECTS DATA ON THE COMMERCIALLY FISHED CRAB SPECIES IN THE SHETLAND ISLANDS, THE UK'S MOST NORTHERLY ISLANDS. Based in Scalloway, Scotland, Shelly surveys crab stocks along the Shetland coastlines and also on fishing boats out at sea. Her research is carried out back in the laboratory.

FISHERIES BIOLOGIST
SHELLY TALLACK

A day in the life of a
FISHERIES BIOLOGIST

Research into the Shetland crab populations is helping Scottish fishermen maintain local crab stocks for future years of fishing.

Crab tagging
Shelly tags each crab by threading a numbered plastic disc on nylon thread through its exoskeleton (shell).

Tagging tools

Pliers   Piercer   Numbered plastic discs

Plastic gear box
Shelly keeps oilskins and rubber boots in a waterproof box. They can be really smelly at the end of a day's fishing!

Today, Shelly plans to join a two-man crew in a commercial crab and lobster fishing boat to sample the crab stocks off the island of Foula. Back on dry land, she will record the day's data on a computer.

4:30am The alarm breaks into my sleep, and I stumble out of bed. Luckily, I packed all my gear and equipment the night before. I make a flask of hot coffee, grab my packed lunch, and load everything into the car. As it's summer, it never quite gets dark in Shetland, so the 45-minute drive to the pier, where I meet today's skipper, is in daylight.

6:00am The fishing boat sets off for one of Shetland's more isolated islands, Foula, where we see many nesting seabirds, including puffins, around the high cliffs.

7:00am We locate a brightly colored buoy that marks the spot where the fishermen's creels – robust traps for catching crabs and lobsters – were set yesterday. Up to 40 creels are attached to one long length of rope called a leader. The fishermen haul in the leader using a hydraulic winch. One by one, they empty the crabs out of the creels, return any bycatch (unwanted catch) to the sea, then rebait the creels with fresh or frozen fish scraps from local fish processors. Once the creels are ready, the leader will be lowered back into the water, down to 30 fathoms – 200 ft (60 m) – and left overnight.

8:00am With fishing underway, I start work on gathering my crab data. As crabs are emptied out of the creels, I select specimens for examination. Because of the wet conditions, I have to write on waterproof paper. First, I record the species type – local crab species include brown or edible crabs, velvet swimming crabs, and shore or green crabs. I note the crab's

Baiting creels
A fisherman baits a creel with fish scraps.

> *Seafood is under increasing demand worldwide, so monitoring the populations fished is vital work.*

Rocky coast
The Shetland Islands have a rugged coastline with narrow, rocky bays called voes.

sex and its reproductive condition – females are sometimes berried (carrying eggs or spawn). Finally, I measure the width of the crab's carapace (shell-like back) using a measuring tool called callipers.

Sea urchin

Starfish

Unwanted bycatch
The creels also capture sea urchins, starfish, scorpion fish, conger eels, and octopuses, which are released back into the sea.

If the crab is big enough, I put it into the fisherman's catch box. However, any crabs that are under the legal minimum landing size (MLS) for their species are returned to the sea. For instance, around Shetland the MLS is set at a width measurement of 5.5 in (140 mm) across the carapace for brown crabs. I put some of the crabs that are under the legal MLS size to one side for tagging later on.

10:00am While the fishermen are busy repairing holes in the creel mesh, I start tagging crabs. First, I pierce two holes through the crab's exoskeleton (shell), then I thread through a length of braided nylon, slip on a small, green plastic disc tag, and finally tie a reef knot. Before releasing the crab back into the sea, I record the tag number, crab size and sex, and our position using the boat's navigation system called the GPS (Global Positioning System). In the future, if this crab is recaptured, I will be able to tell how far it has migrated and how much it has grown.

12:00pm We all break for lunch. I try not to drink too much, as there's no bathroom on board! We continue with our work for another couple of hours. Then the fishermen steer the boat back to the pier.

Berried crab
This velvet swimming crab is carrying about 275,000 eggs.

4:00pm Back on dry land, I thank the fishermen for their help and head back in the car to my laboratory in Scalloway. I have a new berried female to put in the wet lab, which is a large tank with running seawater for holding live crab specimens. Tomorrow, I will start the job of counting her eggs under the microscope – amazingly, there can be as many as three million!

5:00pm I feed the crabs in the tank with mussels, which are their favorite meal! I notice that a young crab has molted (outgrown) its old shell. This is valuable growth data, and it makes my day. I measure the shell size increase, which is dramatic. As the new shell is still soft, I separate this crab from the others. This will protect it until its new exoskeleton hardens.

7:00pm After dinner, I have to enter all the new biological data into my computer database. After three years of researching Shetland's crab populations, I will submit a final report to the Shetland Fishermen's Association and the Shetland Shellfish Management Organization. My findings and recommendations will help them to decide if any fishery controls, such as the minimum landing size or nonfishing areas, need to be changed or added.
These regulations are crucial management tools aimed at sustaining the local crab stocks for future years of fishing.

SHETLAND ISLANDS

Foula

Scalloway

Fishing waters
Fishing takes place all around Shetland's inshore waters, but today's trip is to Foula.

UNITED KINGDOM

Measuring crab sizes
Shelly measures the width of each crab's shell with her callipers.

FOOD FOR TOMORROW

FARMING METHODS NEED TO CHANGE IF WE WANT TO PROTECT THE ENVIRONMENT AND GROW ENOUGH HEALTHY FOOD TO FEED THE world. Scientists are already developing crops that can survive drought or resist pests. This research combined with more natural ways of farming will help people take better care of the land and its wildlife in the future.

66 Highly intensive organic farming can get very close to, and sometimes equal, the yield levels of high-tech agriculture. **99**

PATRICK HOLDEN
SOIL ASSOCIATION

Hydroponic farming enables farmers to grow crops without soil. These lettuces (main picture) are growing in a bed of gravel fed by chemicals dissolved in water. However, more and more people are concerned about the safety of new farming methods. The small picture shows a protester destroying a trial plot of genetically modified (GM) crops.

Seeds and

Since the beginning of

agriculture, about 10,000 years ago,
farmers have been improving their crops and
livestock. They would save the seeds from their best crop
plants and sow them the next year, or select the meatiest
cattle and use these animals for breeding. Each plant and
animal contains genes – sets of chemical instructions for
determining characteristics such as size, weight, or color –
and these genes are passed on from generation to
generation. Today, farmers' breeding programs
continue to produce new and improved crop
varieties and animal breeds.

Multicolored wild corn cobs look quite
different from the large, yellow-seeded
cobs sold in the shops.

Wild crop varieties

The wild ancestors of the cereals,
fruits, and vegetables we buy
today still grow in their native lands.
In Peru, for example, farmers grow more
than 50 varieties of potatoes, and dozens
of varieties of corn. These native crop
ancestors are important to our future.
If modern crops are hit by new diseases,
we will need the genes of their wild
ancestors to breed new, stronger varieties.

World seed banks

To preserve the world's natural
variety of living plants and animals
(biodiversity), scientists are building
up collections of seeds. The plant seeds
can be kept for up to 100 years in cold
storage. These seed banks are used for
research, and help plant breeders create
new crops to feed the world's people.

Wild wheat
This wild grass has
small heads and
grains of wheat.

Durum wheat
This modern, large-
grained wheat
variety is grown to
provide the flour
for pasta.

Wheat's wild origins

Cereals belong to the grass
family. The spindly, wild
ancestors of wheat had small
grains that dropped as soon
as they ripened. Later varieties
were bred to have bigger
seeds. These made more flour,
and stayed on the ear longer
so less grain was lost during
harvesting. Modern wheat
has shorter stems, which suffer
less wind damage in the fields.

Emmer
The main cereal
crop in Roman
times, emmer had
bigger seeds than
its wild ancestor.

Breeds

The last aurochs, the wild ancestor of modern cattle, died on a Polish game reserve in 1627

Choice and variety

Britain's orchards once grew hundreds of varieties of apples and pears. Today, most stores only sell about six of the most profitable and reliable varieties. However, there is a growing demand from consumers for wider choice. This is encouraging fruit producers to grow more unusual and traditional varieties for the local market.

Highland
A hardy, old breed that can survive on cold rain-swept hillsides.

Just 15 different food plants provide most of the world's diet

Hereford
This breed gives more meat and is farmed in 50 countries.

Aberdeen Angus
These cattle provide fine steaks and are bred to grow quickly to adult size.

Sheep breeds

Farmers worldwide keep more than 1.2 billion sheep and goats for their meat, milk, and wool. Different breeds suit different environments. This herd of Romneys is well-suited to the mild climate in New Zealand, whereas long-eared Awassis sheep can withstand the heat of dry, Middle Eastern deserts.

Jacob sheep
This ancient breed, known in biblical times, provides good meat and wool.

Crossbreeding animals

Livestock breeders create new kinds of cattle, sheep, pigs, and poultry by mixing the genes of different breeds. A cattle farmer, for example, might create a dual-purpose breed by crossing the male (bull) of a breed providing good meat, with the female (cow) of another that produces good milk.

DAIRY FARM MANAGER
JAMIE TAIT-JAMIESON

JAMIE TAIT-JAMIESON IS THE MANAGER OF AN ORGANIC DAIRY FARM IN MANAWATU, NEW ZEALAND. AN IMPORTANT PART OF JAMIE'S JOB IS TO MAKE SURE that the conditions are right for healthy pasture growth. This means that the cows in his care always have plenty to eat and are able to produce fresh, nutritious milk.

A day in the life of a
DAIRY FARM MANAGER

Organic dairy farming involves caring for the environment, the welfare of the herd, and also the health of consumers.

Organic farmland
The farm is situated on the banks of the Manawatu River in the North Island of New Zealand. The climate is mild all year round with good rainfall.

Teamworkers
A team of three farm workers, including Jamie's wife and daughter, help him with the twice daily milking and calf-feeding routine.

Jamie manages a team of three farm workers who help with the day-to-day running of the farm. They work in shifts to handle milking the cows and feeding the calves twice a day, every day of the year.

6:00am The day starts at sunrise for the milkers and me. First, we gather for a cup of tea, then we head off to the paddock (field) where our herd of 130 Holstein Friesian cows are starting to wake up. I gently wake them by clapping my hands. We try to keep the cows as calm as

Milking time
The cows stand patiently while the milk is gently sucked from their udders. Jamie wears a plastic apron when carrying out the milking.

possible, which helps them to remain healthy and stress-free. The cows are walked quietly from the paddock to the milking shed. It is important that the cows are not rushed or allowed to bunch up too close to each other. They all have sharp horns, which could cause an injury. The cows walk one by one onto a rotary milking platform where 16 cows can be milked at a time. I put the milking cups onto the four teats of each cow's udder. The warm milk is gently sucked from the cow by the cups, which move in a similar fashion to the

sucking motion of a calf's mouth. By the time the platform has made one slow rotation, the cows have given all their milk. My daughter Mara removes the milking cups from the cows' udders and leads them off the milking platform.

7:30am The milk is stored in a refrigerated vat, where it is cooled down to 39.2°F (4°C). Later, I will transport the fresh, chilled milk to the farm factory where it is turned into yogurt. The

Unloading silage
Changes in the weather need to be taken into account when choosing the right time to harvest surplus grass to make silage.

yogurt is sold in supermarkets throughout New Zealand and is in demand because it is organically produced.

8:00am Once all the cows have been milked, the herd is taken to a fresh paddock, and the cowshed and yards are washed clean of cow

number tag

Feeding time
Calves are always eager to feed on the warm milk brought to them in the calfeteria after milking.

manure with a high-pressure hose. The wastewater runs along a drain and into a settling pond. The pond is home to wild ducks and swans. The cow manure settles at the bottom of the drain, and once a year I clean it out with a digger. The manure is spread over the area that will become the next season's vegetable garden.

9:00am Our next task is to feed the 20 calves. During milking, some of the warm milk is loaded into the calfeteria (a feeding container). I use the farm car to pull it into the paddock where the calves scramble to get ahold of a rubber teat and suck on the milk. We treat many of the calves like pets and give them names such as Pickle, Dot, and Lottie. Mostly though, they are known by the number tag which is placed in their ear at birth.

10:30am After breakfast, I take the tractor and trailer and load it with silage from the stack. Silage is grass that has been harvested in late spring and is used as extra feed in the winter months. As the chopped grass is piled up, a heavy tractor is driven back and forth over it to force out all the air. The stack is covered with plastic sheeting, and the grass is left to heat up and ferment. This process turns the grass into silage, which has a strong, sweet smell. The cows love to eat it, and some of them get very excited when they see the silage tractor. They jump high in the air and kick out their front and back legs! The silage trailer automatically throws the silage out onto rows in the field.

11:30am After feeding the cows and making sure that they are content for the day, I think about the other farm jobs that need to be done. I spend an hour checking and repairing any damaged gates or fences around the fields.

2:00pm Once lunch is over, I go to check on one of the cows with an udder infection to make sure that she is eating and drinking. We use homeopathic medicines to treat any sick cows in the herd. The vet is called when there is a

Number tags
All calves are tagged in the ear at birth with a lifetime identification number.

problem that we can't deal with ourselves. Antibiotics are only used on those animals that would die without them. If a cow gets an antibiotic, it is held in a quarantine paddock for three to four weeks. After this time, the cow rejoins the herd, but her milk is not used for another 12 months. This is the strict guarantee offered to customers, who do not want any antibiotic residue in their organic milk.

3:00pm It is time to start the evening milking and the calf feeding again. The cows in the herd need milking twice a day, 365 days a year because our customers want to buy fresh milk products whenever they go grocery shopping. I am responsible for ensuring that we have new cows calving all year round to maintain an even milk supply.

6:00pm By the time the sun sets, the day's work on the farm is done. I look forward to getting some refreshing sleep.

" Buying organic food helps support farmers who have adopted environmentally friendly methods of production. "

Fresh pastures
After every milking, the cows are taken to a new paddock where they can graze on fresh grass.

GM benefits

The corn in this field looks the same as any other, but it has been given extra genes (genetically modified) to make it resistant to an all-purpose weedkiller. This means that instead of spraying the crop several times with different herbicides, the farmer can spray the field just once. The weeds are killed, and the crop remains unharmed. By reducing the use of chemicals, GM technology can benefit the environment.

GM Food Debate

> "Biotechnology will be a key factor in improving the quality and quantity of the food supply."
>
> JOHN WOOD
> UK FOOD AND DRINK FEDERATION

Scientists can now alter the characteristics of crops by splicing genes from one plant into a totally unrelated plant – something that cannot be done by traditional plant breeding. With this new biotechnology, scientists hope to create genetically modified (GM) crops that will be naturally resistant to insect pests and diseases, grow in very dry soils, contain more food energy or vitamins, or simply taste better and stay fresh longer. But GM technology has created a stormy debate. While some people believe it could help solve world hunger, others are concerned about its possible harmful effects on people and the environment.

Changing nature

This scientist is studying a genetically modified tomato plant in a research laboratory. In one type of GM tomato, scientists have altered the genes that cause overripe fruit to wrinkle and go soft. The modified fruits stay firm, fresh, and appetizing for much longer than ordinary tomatoes.

GM risks

One of the main concerns people have about GM crops is food safety and the possible harmful effects on human health. Others fear that pollen from GM crops might be carried by the wind or insects and cross-pollinate with GM-free crops and wild plants of the same species. More field trials are needed before scientists can be sure that GM crops will be safe in the environment.

❝ I'm Mike from Exton, Pennsylvania. I believe that we should research GM food because it has great potential to help mankind, but it is not yet perfected and should not be marketed until it's 100 percent safe. I'm concerned that new foods could cause allergies and other health risks. Another danger is that GM "super crops" may crossbreed and create "super weeds," which could wipe out other native plants. The release of these GM foods could do more harm than good if they are not completely safe. ❞

Mike Barry

GM corn needs far less spraying with chemicals to control weeds in the crop.

Bees and other insects might carry pollen from GM plants to other plants, and alter them too.

Food research

The addition of long-life genes to these tomatoes will hopefully help to reduce food waste. In other tests, scientists have added the vitamin A gene to a variety of rice grown in Asia. This should help local people, who suffer blindness through lack of this vitamin in their diet. Other laboratories are working on drought-resistant crops to help farmers in the dry regions of Africa, who are plagued by lack of rainfall.

Clear labels

GM soybeans and corn are already on sale in stores in some processed foods. Many people believe that GM foods need clear labels so that consumers can choose whether or not to buy these products. GM developments aim to make food easier to pack, store, and transport. Imagine how convenient it would be, if we could produce square fruit!

❝ I believe the risks to the environment, human health, and agriculture are irreversible. ❞

DR. SUE MEYER
GENEWATCH

World protest

All around the world, people are protesting that GM foods are being introduced too quickly, without enough testing to ensure that they are safe. Many people are also worried that patents (ownership rights) on GM crops will give big biotechnology companies too much power. They are demanding that governments bring in tighter controls.

WATER

People in many parts of the world are desperately short of water, and the problem is getting worse. Wasteful use of water and poorly planned crop watering (irrigation) programs are having a devastating effect on communities and the environments they depend on. People need clean, fresh water to drink. They need water for sanitation, and for their crops and livestock. Droughts cannot be prevented, but even small amounts of rainfall can go a long way if they are carefully collected and stored.

Precious resource

For many people living in West Africa, the only place to collect fresh drinking water is from the village well – where it is pumped from deep underground. The water in open wells and surface streams is often polluted by animal and human waste. Thanks to international aid, many wells are drilled to provide communities with clean, healthy water.

"About 20 percent of the world's population lacks access to safe drinking water."

EARTHSCAN 2000, UNITED NATIONS
ENVIRONMENT PROGRAM

Vanished livelihoods
Aral Sea fishing boats lie stranded due to a failed irrigation program.

Asia's dying lake

The Aral Sea in western Asia was one of the world's largest lakes. But large-scale desert irrigation projects built by Russia in the 1960s diverted the rivers that used to feed it. Today, the lake has lost two-thirds of its water. The surrounding farmland has returned to desert. Salt flats cover the dried-up lake bed, and the local fisheries have been ruined.

CRISIS

Poisoned land

For more than 30 years, billions of gallons of water have been drawn from Pakistan's Indus River to feed farm irrigation programs. Now an ecological disaster threatens. Much of the farmland has been turned into infertile salt flats. These are formed when mineral salts in the soil are drawn up to the surface as water evaporates. This rock-hard layer is toxic to plants and too hard to plow.

Rainfall harvesting techniques in **the dry** regions of **India** have **revived** the Arvari River

SALT FLAT FORMATION

EXPERIMENT

You will need: clean plastic dish or take-out food tray, table salt, rubber gloves, soil, pitcher of water, magnifying glass.

1 PLACE ABOUT ½ in (1 cm) of salt in the dish and cover with 2 in (5 cm) of soil. Press the soil down firmly.

2 WATER THE SOIL until it is wet through. Leave the dish on a warm, sunny windowsill. When the soil dries out, water it again. Repeat this process for two weeks.

3 CHECK THE SOIL surface with a magnifying glass each day. After a few days, tiny salt crystals will appear. After two weeks, the whole surface of the soil will be covered in a hard, salty crust.

This shows that: irrigation water can dissolve salts in the ground, draw them to the surface, and leave them there as the water evaporates.

Always wash your hands after handling soil.

Saving water

New cultivation methods, such as hydroponics, allow farmers to feed and water their greenhouse crops with much less waste. Tomato plants are grown without soil in bags filled with gravel. Just the right amounts of water containing nutrients can be pumped through the gravel directly to the plant roots.

Crop circles

The crops in these fields in Oregon are grown in circles to suit the irrigation method used by the farmer. When rainfall is scarce, a long water pipe, supported by sets of wheels with soft tires to protect the soil, moves around a central point and sprays the crop as it goes.

Rainfall harvesting

Low earth- or stone-wall dams, called johads, are built on sloping farmland in India. They hold back precious rainwater and help it soak into the ground. Crops can draw on the stored water even through dry periods.

AGRICULTURAL ADVISER
GÖTZ DANIEL

GÖTZ DANIEL WORKS AS AN ADVISER FOR AN ASSOCIATION OF ORGANIC AGRICULTURE, BASED IN SCHLESWIG-HOLSTEIN IN NORTHERN GERMANY. Götz offers specialist advice to farmers on how they can improve their organic farming methods, avoid the use of pesticides and fertilizers, and help to conserve nature.

A day in the life of an
AGRICULTURAL ADVISER

Thanks to specialist advice, farmers in Germany are adopting organic methods to ensure the conservation of local wildlife.

Organic farming region
Götz has his office base in Bordesholm and makes visits to organic farmers throughout the region of Schleswig-Holstein.

Visual aid
This picture wheel helps Götz explain crop rotation to farmers.

Today Götz plans to spend the morning at work in his office and the afternoon out on farm visits. One farmer wants some advice on how to build an environmentally friendly pigsty. Another is looking for a more ecological way to manage his fields.

8:00am My day begins with office work. Several farmers phone me in the morning to ask questions about organic agriculture. When I'm out on the road, I can still be contacted about urgent matters by mobile phone. However, it's easier to deal with questions in the office, where I have my computer data and a library of books on organic agriculture. Each month, my association produces a magazine on

Wildlife homes
Piles of stones placed at the edges of fields provide an ideal habitat for snakes, lizards, and spiders.

Grass snake

organic agriculture for its members. All the advisers are required to write articles for it. I am responsible for providing information on nature-based pig farming, the farming of organic crops, and nature conservation. My colleagues are experts in the fields of market gardening, and cattle and chicken farming.

9:00am I start writing an article on how farmers can best spare frogs unnecessary suffering when they are mowing their meadows to provide hay for cows in the winter. Many farmers use a machine that works like a big lawnmower to cut the grass. Unfortunately, the swiftly rotating blade not only cuts the grass, but it also slices up many frogs and other small animals such as grasshoppers. This problem has led to storks becoming less plentiful in the region, as they feed mainly on frogs. My article explains to farmers how it is preferable to use mowers with special blades that let them cut the grass more carefully. By using blades that are made up of lots of small scissors the grass is not mown so short. The frogs can hide deep down in the grass and find some protection from the blades.

Common frog
Farmers are helping to protect frog populations.

Pond life
By maintaining the ponds in their fields, farmers can provide homes to frogs and many different types of insects.

> 66 If farmers want to farm in a way that will preserve our environment for the future, they must work with nature rather than against it. 99

10:30am I start to research information for a second article that will examine the feeding of organic pigs. Pigs should be given food that is both tasty and healthy. This ensures that they grow at a reasonable pace without getting too fat.

Organic pig rearing
Some organic pig farmers rear their pigs in free-range units.

My article will describe how breeders can mix various ingredients together to feed both small and large pigs in this way. The feed ingredients – grain, peas, field beans, and clover – are all crops that can be grown on the farm itself without being sprayed with chemical pesticides or fertilizers.

11:30am A farmer phones up to inquire about the best sowing time for a good crop of organic field beans. I explain how field beans should be sown at the beginning of March for an early harvest.

Animal pathways
Paths running alongside hedges are routes that wild animals, such as the red fox, can use.

If the crop flowers early, they are less likely to be infested with aphids (greenflies), which tend to thrive later on in the year. As organic farmers do not use chemical pesticides, pests such as aphids have to be avoided in a different way. Early planting is one method of achieving this. I also suggest that the farmer plants just half of his field with beans and sows peas in the other half to reduce the

risk of crop failure from aphid damage. In this way, he should be guaranteed a good healthy yield of both these organic crops.

Vital hedges
Hedges provide habitat protection for wild animals and plants, which is important for the conservation of nature.

12:30pm After a short lunch break, I drive to a farm to talk to an organic pig farmer about how to construct a new pigsty. The old sty is dark and rather cramped. The farmer would like to build a new sty with room for more pigs. I recommend that he try for a sty with partially open walls. This would not need to be heated, since pigs like to build themselves a warm nest out of straw to sleep in during the cold weather. Sties like this save on energy and therefore help to prevent unnecessary pollution of the environment.

4:30pm On the way home I visit a second farmer. We discuss how he could do more for nature and the wild animals and plants that inhabit his fields and farmland. The farmer has a very large field situated between two woods. I suggest that he split this field in two by planting a hedge of different types of bushes which

would provide a vital link between the two areas of woodland. Hedges made up of different plants have many positive side effects on nature. Many insects, such as ladybugs and hoverflies, and animals, including birds, frogs, hedgehogs, and foxes like to make their homes in

Bird conservation
Woodland conservation helps to maintain the populations of local birds, such as the yellow hammer.

hedges. In addition, a hedge acts like a corridor for animals wanting to travel from one woodland area to another. This farmer talks about the possibility of planting one with the help of local schoolchildren.

6:30pm Back at home, I take a short break for supper. Then I spend a further hour on the computer reading and answering emails from fellow advisers in organic agriculture. I also surf the internet for new literature and information on the links between nature conservation and organic agriculture.

Protecting wildlife

Many crop farmers leave a wide band of natural vegetation around the edge of their fields. Along with hedges, trees, and woods, these pesticide-free wildlife reserves are rich in the grasses and flowers that provide food sources and shelter for insects, birds, and animals.

Frogs
Populations of frogs help farmers to control slugs – a major crop pest.

Hedgehogs
In natural areas, hedgehogs flourish and prey on slugs and insects.

Birds
Thrushes and other birds thrive on wild areas of farmland, where they feed on snails and insects.

Working with Nature

ACTION! GO ORGANIC

Start a compost heap at home to save on plant fertilizer and improve the soil in your garden.

See what organic foods are available in your local supermarket. Meat and dairy products can be organic, too.

Many farmers in the developed world are turning away from using pesticides and fertilizers and are growing food more naturally. Organic farming produces smaller harvests than intensive farming and, as a result, produce can be more expensive. However, some consumers are happy to pay a bit extra in return for chemical-free foods. Farmers in developing countries with poor soils can also increase their food production by growing combinations of crops. This farming method protects the land by putting nutrients back into the soil, and also conserves the environment.

Animal manure can be sprayed from a tank mounted on a tractor.

Recycling natural fertilizers

Farmers often keep animals and spread their manure on the land. This is a natural source of nitrogen and other chemicals that crops need for healthy growth. Soil fertility can also be improved by digging in composted plant remains and growing a mixture of crops in a rotation system.

Farming with trees

In hot climates, where the Sun can dry out the soil and scorch young crops, many farmers are choosing to grow trees in their fields. This system is called agroforestry. Rows of papaya trees provide excellent shade and wind protection for this field of corn (maize) in Polynesia. The farmer can harvest fruit from the trees as well as his cereal crop.

Papaya fruit

NATURAL RECYCLING

You will need: 1 red pepper, knife, polyethylene food bag, bag tie

1 CUT THE PEPPER in half. Use one half for the experiment and leave it uncovered for a few hours. This will allow microscopic mold spores in the air to land on the soft inner surface of the pepper.

2 PLACE THE PEPPER inside a bag and seal it with a bag tie. Leave the bag in a warm place.

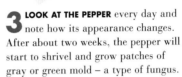

3 LOOK AT THE PEPPER every day and note how its appearance changes. After about two weeks, the pepper will start to shrivel and grow patches of gray or green mold – a type of fungus.

This shows that: when a plant dies, the remains are quickly broken down by fungi, bacteria, and other tiny organisms. In nature, this rotting process returns all the plant's nutrients to the soil.

> "Wildlife is not a luxury for the organic farmer, but an essential part of the farming system."
> SOIL ASSOCIATION

Organic food sales are growing faster than any other area of the food market

Rearing ducks in rice paddies helps to control insect pests.

Animal helpers

Many Chinese rice farmers also raise ducks and geese for their eggs and meat. They keep the birds in flooded rice paddies, where they eat weeds and insect larvae (grubs). The bird droppings fertilize the fields. Some Asian farmers stock their rice paddies with fish as an extra source of food.

Double crop benefits

Farmers can improve poor soils by "intercropping." This means growing one crop alongside a different crop. Here, spring wheat produces grain. The alternating rows of beans provide food, plus leaves for animal feed. They also improve the soil by producing nitrogen – a natural fertilizer.

Action Plan

IF YOU CARE ABOUT FOOD AND FARMING issues and want to help save the planet's natural environment, there are many organizations that will help to get you involved. This list includes those you can contact in the US, as well as international organizations you can visit on the internet.

American Bird Conservancy
Dedicated to the conservation of wild birds and their habitats. This website has information and campaigns about current issues such as the effect of climate change on birds.

www.abcbirds.org

PO Box 249
The Plains, VA 20198

Environment Canada
A federal department dedicated to preserving and enhancing the quality of Canada's natural environment, including water, air, and soil quality, as well as conserving Canada's renewable resources.

www.ec.gc.ca

315 St. Joseph Boulevard
Hull, PQ, K1A 0H3
Canada

Environmental Investigation Agency
An international campaigning organization committed to improving conservation laws – and making sure that existing laws are upheld.

www.eia-international.org

PO Box 53343
Washington, DC 20009

Environmental Protection Agency
A US government agency that works to safeguard the environment and protect human health. Visit the EPA website for information on a wide range of environmental topics, including details about pesticides and food safety.

www.epa.gov

Farm Sanctuary
A US-based organization that operates farm animal sanctuaries and campaigns to stop the exploitation of farm animals.

www.farmsanctuary.org

PO Box 150
Watkins Glen, NY 14891

and

PO Box 1065
Orland, CA 95963

Food and Agriculture Organization of the United Nations (FAO)
The UN agency founded in 1945 that works to alleviate world poverty and hunger, improve nutrition, and promote agricultural and rural developments that conserve the environment.

www.fao.org

Friends of the Earth
An international network of environmental groups that commissions research and campaigns for changes in the law.

www.foe.org

1025 Vermont Ave, NW
3rd floor
Washington, DC 20005-6303

and

www.foecanada.org

206-260 St. Patrick Street
Ottawa, ON, K1N 5K5
Canada

Greenpeace
One of the world's leading environmental organizations, involved in direct action to safeguard the planet's future.

www.greenpeace.org

702 H Street, NW
Washington, DC 20001

and

www.greenpeacecanada.org

250 Dundas St W, Suite 605
Toronto, ON, M5T 2Z5
Canada

Health Canada

A Canadian department responsible for food and drug regulations and for providing the people of Canada with health and nutrition information.

www.healthcanada.net

A.L. 0904A
Ottawa, ON, K1A 0K9
Canada

Heifer Project International

The Heifer Project works with communities who determine their own needs. Donated cows provide a steady milk food source and income. Farmers are trained to manage grazing, plant trees and crops, and use natural fertilizer in ways that improve the environment.

www.heifer.org

PO Box 8058
Little Rock, AR 72203

Médecins Sans Frontières (Doctors without Borders)

An international humanitarian aid organization that provides emergency medical assistance to populations in danger. It also works to improve people's nutrition and health, and collaborates on water and sanitation projects.

www.msf.org

Organic Consumers Association

The Organic Consumers Association is a public interest organization dedicated to building a healthy, safe, and sustainable system of food production and consumption.

www.purefood.org

6101 Cliff Estate Rd,
Little Marais, MN 55614

Oxfam

Oxfam is a development organization and relief agency working to put an end to world poverty and suffering.

www.oxfamamerica.org

733 15th Street NW, Suite 340
Washington, DC 20005

Sea Shepherd Conservation Society

An organization devoted to conserving and protecting life in the oceans. Has its own fleet of boats which investigate illegal fishing and whaling.

www.seashepherd.org

PO Box 2616
Friday Harbor
WA 98250

Sierra Club

One of America's leading environmental organizations. The Sierra Club campaigns to protect wildlife, wilderness and unspoiled habitats.

www.sierraclub.org

85 Second Street, Second Floor
San Francisco
CA 94105-3411

United Nations Environment Programme (UNEP)

The UN agency founded to safeguard and enhance the environment for the benefit of present and future generations.

www.unep.org

Willing Workers on Organic Farms (WWOOF)

An international organization that arranges short working breaks on organic farms.

www.phdcc.com/wwoof/wpusa

World Food Programme of the United Nations (WFP)

The front-line food aid organization of the UN helping to feed victims of man-made and natural disasters. The agency also aims to improve the nutrition of vulnerable people worldwide.

www.wfp.org

Worldwide Fund for Nature (WWF)

The world's largest international conservation organization. Visit its website to gain access to fact sheets and campaign information.

www.panda.org

1250 24th Street NW
Washington, DC 20037-1175

Index

Credits

Dorling Kindersley would like to thank:

Amanda Carroll, Robin Hunter, Keith Newell, and Mark Regardsoe for their design help; Lynn Bresler for the index. Steve Gorton for the photography of the experiments, and hand model Emily Gorton.

Thanks also to the Day in the Life experts and their organizations who provided many free photographs: Götz Daniel (Agricultural Adviser), Beth Grafton-Cardwell/ Kearney Agricultural Center, University of California (Entomologist), Henrietta Howard/Médecins Sans Frontières (Nutritionist), Jamie Tait-Jamieson/ Biofarm (Dairy Farm Manager), and Shelly Tallack (Fisheries Biologist).

The author would like to thank: The Pesticide Trust; Rudolf L Schreiber of Pronatur, Germany; the Sea Fish Industry Authority; and the Worldwide Fund for Nature.

Additonal photography: Geoff Brightling, Jane Burton, Martin Cameron, Peter Chadwick, Andy Crawford, Philip Dowell, Neil Fletcher, Steve Gorton, Frank Greenaway, Dave King, Stuart Lafford, Cyril Laubscher, Andrew McRobb, David Murray, Ian O'Leary, Dave Rudkin, Tim Ridley, Karl Shone, Kim Taylor.

Picture Credits

The publishers would like to thank the following for their kind permission to reproduce the photographs:
a = above; c = center; b = bottom; l = left; r = right; t = top; f = far; n = near.

The J. Allan Cash Photolibrary: 31tc.
Bruce Coleman Ltd: 6-7, 24; Gunter Kohler 2-3, 46-47, 62-63; Kim Taylor 52-53; Pacific Stock 57bl.
Corbis UK Ltd: Boca Raton 21cl; David Reed 38bl; George McCarthy 55cl; Jim Richardson 33tl; Jonathan Blair 18tr; Kevin Schafer 43-44; Liba Taylor 19cl; Michael Callan 55tr; Nevada Wier 53tl; Otto Lang 28-29; Roger Ressmeyer 15br. **Centre for Science and Environment, India:** 53bl. **Ecoscene:** Andrew Brown 33tr; Chinch Gryniewicz 27c; Hart 57br; Mike Whittle 57tl. **Environmental Images:** Steve Morgan 11bl. **Garden and Wildlife Matters:** 6tl, 10-11. **Robert Harding Picture Library:** 13cr. **Holt Studios International:** D. Donne Bryant 27bc; Inga Spence 14-15, 21br, 32, 33b, 34tl, 38-39, 46tl; Julia Chalmers 38cb; Mary Taylor 47bl; Michael Major 29tr, 46bl; Nigel Cattlin 7tr, 26-27, 27cl, 34-35b, 34-35t, 44, 53cl, 56br; Sue Llewellyn 29cr. **Hutchison Library:** 16tr, 29tl; Jeremy Horner 27c; Jon Burbank 23b; Philip Wolmuth 22tl. **Image Bank:** 17tl; Michael Melford 53br; Stuart Pee 23cr. **FLPA - Images of Nature:** Alwyn Roberts 39tr; R. Hosking 8-9. **N.H.P.A.:** David Woodfall 56tl. **Planet Earth Pictures:** Thomas Wiewandt 31cl. **Rex Features:** 33cl; Christiana Laruffa 17br; Sipa Press 12tr. **Science Photo Library:** Chris Knapton 50-51; Victor Habbick Visions 51cr. **Still Pictures:** Adrian Arbib 44-45; B & C Alexander 41br; Edward Parker 41bl; Gerard & Margi Moss 15c; Gil Moti 52b; Hartmut Schwarzbach 16-17, 17tr, 17ca; Joerg Boethling 12; Juan Carlos 41tr; Mark Edwards 13tl, 14tl, 20l, 24-25, 40tl, 41tc, 52tl, 58-59; Nick Cobbing 51b; Nigel Dickinson 33tl; Pierre Gleizes 23tl; Robert Holmgren 50b, 51c; Shehzad Noorani 31bl; Thomas Raupach 40b. **Tony Stone Images:** Arnulf Husmo 28tl; Jake Rajs 47tl; Ken Fisher 12-13; Michael Rosenfeld 21bl, 35c; Rex A. Butcher 13tr.

Jacket Credits
Bruce Coleman Ltd: Gunter Kohler front c. **Corbis UK Ltd:** David Reed back cra. **Holt Studios International:** D. Donne Bryant back bc; Nigel Cattlin inside front b. **Hutchison Library:** Jeremy Horner back bl. **FLPA - Images of Nature:** R. Hosking front bc. **Science Photo Library:** Victor Habbick Visions back clb. **Still Pictures:** Gerard & Margi Moss back cla; Nigel Dickinson front bl; Robert Holmgren front br.

2 7/0 6 (03)